ONE HUNDRED FROGS

ONE HUNDRED FROGS

BY HIROAKI SATO

ILLUSTRATIONS BY J. C. BROWN

Inklings

First edition, 1995

Published by Weatherhill, Inc., 568 Broadway, Suite 705, New York, NY 10012.
Protected by copyright under terms of the International Copyright Union; all rights reserved. Except for fair use in book reviews, no part of this book may be reproduced for any reason by any means, including any method of photographic reproduction, without permission of the publisher. Printed in the United States.

Library of Congress Cataloging in Publication Data

Sato, Hiroaki, 1942–
    One hundred frogs / by Hiroaki Sato. –1st ed.
        p.   cm.
    Translations of a famous haiku by Matsuo Bashō, and others about a frog jumping into a pond.
    ISBN 0-8348-0335-6
1. Matsuo, Bashō, 1644–1694—Translations into English.
2. Haiku—Translations into English.
I. Title.
PL794.4.A6 1995
895.6'132—dc20   94-48328
                                            CIP

4

CONTENTS

ONE HUNDRED FROGS

Introduction

During the Edo period (1603-1868), amateur Zen proselytizers are said to have made the rounds of inns and villages giving sermons on the profundities of certain haiku—then called *hokku*—to make a living. One such haiku was, scholars say, by Uejima Onitsura (1661-1738):

> *Teizen ni shiroku saitaru tsubaki kana*
> In the garden blooming white are camellias

and another was one by Matsuo Bashō (1644–94):

> *Furuike ya kawazu tobikomu mizu no oto*
> An old pond: a frog jumps into the water the sound

Of these two, Onitsura's piece is intentionally Zen: it has a headnote written by the poet himself: "Monk Kūdō asked me, 'What's your *haikai* eye like?' I replied on the spot." The allusion here is to Case Thirty-seven of the *Mumonkan* (The Gateless Gate), a canonical Zen text. The case reads, in part, "The student said, 'What is the meaning of the Patriarch coming from the West?' The master said, 'Oak trees in the garden in front of us.' "

The "Patriarch" is Bodhidarma (c. 470–543), known in Japan as Daruma, an Indian monk who traveled to China around 520 and established Zen there. Asking "What is the meaning of the Patriarch coming from the West?" is the same as asking "What is Zen?" The "master" is Chao-chou, a Chinese Zen patriarch who was born in 778 and died in 897.[1] Finally, *haikai* means "humor," and when applied, as in this instance, to the sequential poetic form of renga, of which the *hokku* was the opening part, it means rejection of poetic diction in favor of down-to-earth expression.

Though associated with the same Chao-chou story, the Zen provenance of Bashō's haiku is less certain. Indeed, the assessments of Bashō's friends suggest that his five-seven-five syllables were intended or taken as

an example of *haikai* twisting. As Kagami Shikō (1665–1731), who joined Bashō's group in 1690, tells it in his *Kuzu no Matsubara* (Pine Grove with Kudzu), one spring day Bashō was sitting around with a couple of friends, when he heard frogs plopping into the pond outside. He then came up with the seven-five syllables, *kawazu tobikomu mizu no oto*, "the sound of frogs leaping in the water." One of his companions, Enomoto Kikaku[2] (1661–1707), suggested *yamabuki ya* for the first five syllables. The *yamabuki* (*Kerria japonica*), commonly known as yellow rose, was a plant to be associated with frogs in traditional poetry. Bashō thought for a while and then chose instead a phrase rarely used at the time, *furuike*, "old pond." It was the sort of literary twisting that *haikai* masters like Bashō lived by.

Allow me to backtrack somewhat.

Word for word, *furuike* is a noun made from the adjective *furushi* (old) and the noun *ike* (pond, pool, or mere) and means a pond that has been around for a time, but not necessarily, as some might imagine, a puddle of algal goo. *Ya*, in this instance, is a *kireji*, a cutting or separating particle. Much has been said and written about *kireji* because the five-seven-five-syllable *hokku*, though part of a longer form, was, from the outset, expected to be able to stand on its own as an independent verse, and a *kireji* was thought to be an effective means of helping achieve that independence. By Bashō's time, indeed, eighteen *kireji*—*ya* and *kana* prominent among them—had officially been recognized. Perhaps taking into account the perception that *kireji* also add poetic overtones, Harold J. Isaacson has observed of three of them that "they have the meaning that lies in themselves as sounds, and in that way are as meaningful when set in the English translation as they are in the Japanese."[3] Bashō himself refused to ascribe special meanings or functions to select particles and simply said, "Every sound unit is a *kireji*."

Kawazu (frog) can be either singular or plural because, as here, the Japanese language often fails to make numerical distinctions. Singular or plural, *kawazu* is the subject of the verb that follows, *tobikomu* (to jump, leap in)—here, as happens in Japanese grammar, at once conclusive and participial. The final five syllables, *mizu no oto* (water's sound or noise) are not, as sometimes translated, onomatopoeic. (In one of his parodies of

Bashō in the seventeen-syllable form, the Zen master Sengai [1751–1837] wrote: *Furuike ya nani yara pon to tobikonda*, "An old pond: something has jumped in with a plop." Here, *pon to*, "with a plop," is onomatopoeic.)

Bashō's *hokku* comes with a *wakiku*—the second, seven-seven-syllable unit in a *renga* sequence—attributed to Kikaku. Together they read:

Furuike ya kawazu tobikomu mizu no oto
An old pond: a frog jumps in the water the sound

ashi no wakaba ni kakaru kumo no su
suspended over young rush blades a spider's web

If Bashō and his friends composed the remaining thirty-four of the standard thirty-six-unit sequence or ninety-eight of the orthodox one-hundred-unit sequence, they have not survived. Regardless, this *hokku* has since become the most famous piece in the genre, until Masaoka Shiki (1867–1902) was able to say flatly: "Even among those under heaven who don't have the faintest idea what *haikai* is, there is no one who doesn't recite this piece on an old pond, and at the mention of *hokku* they at once think of the old pond." This statement is even truer today, as the haiku form or the notion thereof has spread to a great many countries of the world.

I was initially prompted to collect English translations of the "pond/frog" more than a dozen years ago when my erudite friend Kyoko Selden sent me a list of about twenty, French renditions included, and asked me to guess the translators. What you see following these introductory remarks is the result of the playful collecting that ensued. It is grouped into two sections.

The first section, which originally covered the period up to 1981, consists of the translations found in print and is chronologically arranged.

The greatest contributor to this section is Kondō Tadashi, whose collection of fifty-one for his master's degree William J. Higginson passed on to me along with his own addition of several. Ross Figgins, a haiku bibliographer, sent in thirty. Both Mr. Higginson and Mr. Figgins provided bibliographies, thereby relieving me of an onerous task. The bibliography for this section is included at the end of this booklet.

Since the early 1980s I have naturally seen other translations in various books. Of those, one that deserves mention and inclusion is Makoto Ueda's new version: it comes with comments on the *hokku* by an array of people, from Bashō's contemporaries such as Shikō to modern scholars. As you will note, in his new translation Professor Ueda has replaced the imitative "splash" with "water's sound."

When the initial collection of printed translations was ready, I sent it to my friends and asked for their own translations and variations. The second section is a corpus of their responses, listed alphabetically by author. Since the publication of the whole assemblage more than a decade ago, in *One Hundred Frogs: From Renga to Haiku to English*,[4] I have received several offerings which I might be able to consider adding now were I a more meticulous compiler. But here again, I shall add just one: Stephen Reckert's version. Though it has appeared in his book, it can be added in this section, I think, because when he saw the collection in my earlier book, Professor Reckert took the figurative number "one hundred" as literal and offered his as "version 101":

> The old pond.
> A frog plunges in
> (sound of the water).[5]

In both the original book and this new Inkling edition, the number "one hundred" is used in the Chinese (and therefore Japanese) sense of "many." In fact, the actual compilation lists nearly a hundred-fifty translations and take-offs.

Professor Reckert's placement of *mizu no oto* in parentheses reminds us: Is there any special import to "sound"? My teacher of English, the poet Eleanor Wolff, thinks so, and has pointed to Arthur Avalon's *Serpent*

Power for support.[6] So does Robin Hough, who has shown me various paragraphs of the Upanishads that point to the importance of sound in our universe. As Mr. Hough says, our frog actually puts in an appearance in the sixth *prapathaka*, the twenty-second paragraph, titled in Robert Hume's translation, "Reaching the higher, non-sound Brahma by meditation on the sound 'Om'."[7]

At a more down-to-earth level, David Attenborough has speculated that the first voice on this globe may have come from a frog—a fascinating point that brings us back to Bashō and his haiku.[8] In the orthodox tradition of Japanese poetry, when you mentioned a frog you were supossed to refer to its croaking. Bashō opened a new way to look at our surroundings by breaking this rule: he allowed the batrachian to take a plunge.

Notes

1. That is, he lived for one hundred nineteen years.
2. Also known as Takarai Kikaku.
3. Isaacson, Harold. *Peonies Kana: Haiku by the Upasaka Shiki* (New York: Theatre Arts Books, 1972), xx.
4. Sato, Hiroaki. *One Hundred Frogs: From Renga to Haiku to English* (New York & Tokyo: Weatherhill, 1983).

5. Reckert, Stephen. *Beyond Chrysanthemus: Perspectives on Poetry East and West* (Clarendon Press, 1993), 219.
6. Avalon, Arthur. *Serpent Power* (Madras: Ganesh and Co. Private Ltd., 1957).
7. Hume, Robert Ernest, trans. *The Thirteen Principal Upanishads* (London: Oxford University Press, 1921), 437. " 'Verily, there are two Brahmas to be meditated upon: sound and non-sound. Now, non-sound is revealed only by sound.' Now, in this case the sound-Brahma is *Om*."
8. Attenborough, David. *Life on Earth* (Little, Brown and Company, 1979), 145. "It is intriguing to speculate, as you stand in a swamp listening to this astounding and deafening chorus, that, although much must have changed in the millions of years since the first amphibians appeared, it was nonetheless, an amphibian voice that first sounded over the land which, until then, had heard nothing but the chirps and whirrs of insects."

POEMS

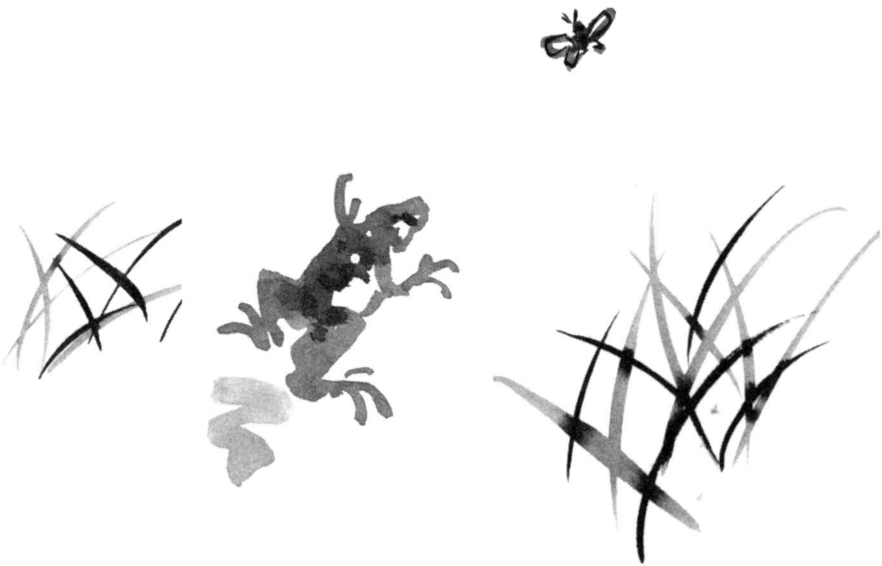

Section One

Masaoka Shiki

> The old mere!
> A frog jumping in
> The sound of water

Lafcadio Hearn

> Old pond—frogs jumped in—sound of water.

W. G. Aston

An ancient pond!
With a sound from the water
Of the frog as it plunges in.

24

Basil Hall Chamberlain

The old pond, aye! and the sound of a frog leaping into the water.

Clara A. Walsh

An old-time pond, from off whose shadowed depth
Is heard the splash where some lithe frog leaps in.

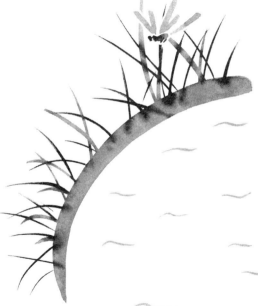

William J. Porter

Stillness

Into the calm old lake
A frog with flying leap goes plop!
  The peaceful hush to break.

Gertrude Emerson

Old pond, aye! and the sound of a frog jumping in.

Yone Noguchi

The old pond!
A frog leapt into—
List, the water sound!

Curtis Hidden Page

A lonely pond in age-old stillness sleeps . . .
   Apart, unstirred by sound or motion . . . till
Suddenly into it a lithe frog leaps.

Inazo Nitobe

Into a old pond
A frog took a sudden plunge,
Then is heard a splash.

John Thomas Bryan

There is the old pond!
  Lo, into it jumps a frog:
hark, water's music!

Asataro Miyamori

The old pond!
  A frog has plunged—
    The splash!

Into the calm old pond
A frog plunged—then the splash.

The Old Pond

The ancient pond!
A frog plunged—splash!

The old pond! A frog plunged—
The sound of the water!

Hidesaburo Saito

Old garden lake!
  The frog thy depth doth seek,
    And sleeping echoes wake.

Minoru Toyoda

An ancient pond!
  A frog leaps in;
The sound of the water!

Harold G. Henderson

An ancient pond;
  Plash of the water
    When a frog jumps in.

Fumiko Saisho

Fu-ru (old) *i-ke* (pond) *ya, ka-wa-zu* (frog) *to-bi-ko-mu*
(jumping into) *mi-zu* (water) *no o-to* (sound)

Inazo Nitobe

An old pond—
A frog jumps in—
A splash of water.

Daisetz T. Suzuki

Into the ancient pond
A frog jumps
Water's sound!

R. H. Blyth

The old pond.
  A frog jumps in—
    Plop!

Kenneth Yasuda

Ancient pond unstirred
Into which a frog has plunged,
  A splash was heard.

R. H. Blyth

The old pond;
A frog jumps in,—
The sound of the water.

G. S. Fraser

The old pond, yes!
A frog jumping in.
The water's noise!

The old pond, yes, and
A frog-jumping-in-the-
Water's noise!

Old pond, yes, and
Frog-jump-in-
Water's noise.

Old pond, yes, and
Frog-jump-in!
Water's noise!

Donald Keene

The ancient pond
A frog leaps in
The sound of the water.

The ancient pond, a frog jumps in, the sound of the water.

Kenneth Rexroth

An old pond—
The sound
Of a diving frog.

42

Peter Beilenson

OLD DARK SLEEPY POOL . . .
QUICK UNEXPECTED
FROG
GOES PLOP! WATERSPLASH!

Nippon Gakujutsu Shinkōkai
(an institution)

The old pond!
A frog jumps in—
Sound of the water.

Harold G. Henderson

Old pond:
 frog jump-in
  water-sound.

Old-pond : frog jump-in : water-sound

Old pond—
 and a frog-jump-in
  water-sound

Anonymous
(as cited in the *Times Literary Supplement*)

Ancient pond;
frog jumps in;
sound of water.

Hiroshi Takamine

Oh, into the old pond
 A frog plunged,
  With a splash!
   (And once again calm prevails!)

Cid Corman

old pond
frog leaping
splash

Daisetz T. Suzuki

The old pond, ah!
A frog jumps in:
The water's sound.

Harold Stewart

The old green pond is silent; here the hop
Of a frog plumbs the evening stillness: plop!

Shunkichi Akimoto

Into the old pond
Leaps a frog
Lo, the sound of the water.

Peter Beilenson and Harry Behn

AN OLD SILENT POND . . .
INTO THE POND
A FROG JUMPS,
SPLASH! SILENCE AGAIN.

Edward G. Seidensticker

The quiet pond
A frog leaps in,
The sound of the water.

Dion O'Donnol

AYE, THE OLD POND AND

A-FROG-THAT-IS-A-LEAPING-IN-THE-WATER

Harry Behn

An old silent pond . . .
A frog jumps into the pond,
    splash! Silence again.

Geoffrey Bownas and Anthony Thwaite

> An old pond
> A frog jumps in—
> Sound of water.

Masaru V. Otake

> The old pond,
> Frog jumps in—
> The sound of water.

Nobuyuki Yuasa

Breaking the silence
Of an ancient pond,
A frog jumped into water—
A deep resonance.

Scott Alexander

By an ancient pond
a bullfrog sits on a rock
waiting for Basho?

Sylvia Cassedy and Kunihiro Suetake

Old pond, blackly still—
frog, plunging into water,
splinters silent air.

Old pond:
frog jump in
water-sound.

Dion O'Donnol

The silent old pond
a mirror of ancient calm,
a frog-leaps-in splash . . .

Anonymous (as cited in *Don't Tell the Scarecrow*)

> The old pond.
> A frog jumps into the water—
> SPLASH.

Edward Bond

> Silent old pool
> Frog jumps
> Kdang!

Cana Maeda

old pond
a frog in-leaping
water-note

G. S. Fraser

The old pond, yes, and
A frog is jumping into
The water, and splash.

Old pond, yes, and
Frog jumping into
The water's noise.

Old pond, yes,
Frog there jumping,
Water's noise.

Armando Martins Janeira

Ah, the old pond
A frog jumps in
Sound of water.

Makoto Ueda

> The old pond—
> A frog leaps in,
> And a splash.

William J. Higginson

> Old pond . . .
> a frog leaps in
> water's sound.

Robert H. Brower

The ancient pond:
A frog jumps in—
The sound of water.

William Howard Cohen

Mossy pond;
frog leaping in—
splash!

Kenjun Ikeda

The old pond!
A frog jumps in
With splash-splosh.

Daniel C. Buchanan

Into the old pond
A frog suddenly plunges.
The sound of water.

Dorothy Britton

> Listen! a frog
> Jumping into the stillness
>   Of an ancient pond!

Joan Giroux

> An old pond
> A frog jumps in
> The sound of the water.

Alfred H. Marks

The old pond:
A frog jumps in,—
The sound of the water

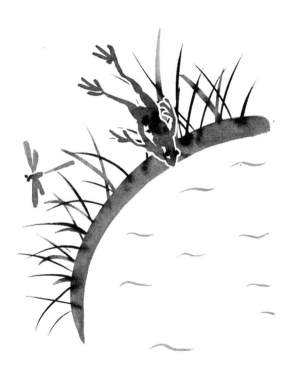

(limerick)

There once was a curious frog
Who sat by a pond on a log
And, to see what resulted,
In the pond catapulted
With a water-noise heard round the bog.

(sonnet)

A frog who would a-water-sounding go
Into some obscure algae-covered pool
had best be sure no poetasting fool
Is waiting in the weeds and, to his woe,
Commemorates his pluck so all will know
His name and lineage, not for the fine school
He learned to sing at, nor, to make men drool
The flavor of his leg from thigh to toe.
He will not for his mother be remembered,
Nor for his father's deeds, his honor bright,
Nor for his brother's leg dismembered,
And eaten by a king with rare delight.
He will be famous simply for the sorta
Noise he makes just when he hits the water.

Basho

Swoop!
Green, bug-eyed, wingless, conquering air,
earth-thrusting legs outstretched in triumph;
descending,
striking,
submerging in jade, groundless depths.
And above
the jet thrown high tumbles,
the shaken air composes to silence;
the rings of water spread, strike shore,
return colliding and subside.

Robert Aitken

Old pond ! / Frog jumps in / Water 's sound

The old pond;
A frog jumps in,—
The sound of water.

The old pond has no walls.
The frog simply jumped in,
And his sound does not echo at all.

Felix-Marti Ibanez

The old pond!
A frog jumps:
Sound of water!

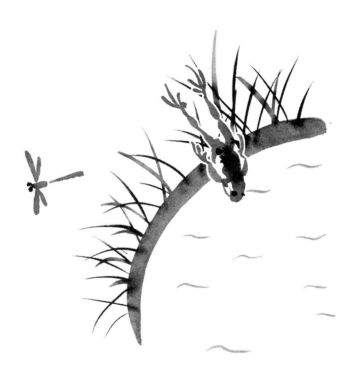

Robert Aitken

The old pond;
A frog jumps in—
The sound of the water.

(word-for-word)

Old pond!
frog jumps in
water of sound

The old pond has no walls;
A frog just jumps in;
Do you say there is an echo?

Lucien Stryk and Takashi Ikemoto

Old pond,
leap-splash—
a frog.

Earl Miner

> The still old pond
> and as a frog leaps in it
> the sound of a splash

Allen Ginsberg

> The old pond
> A frog jumped in,
> Kerplunk!

Earl Miner and Hiroko Odagiri

The old pond is still
a frog leaps right into it
splashing the water

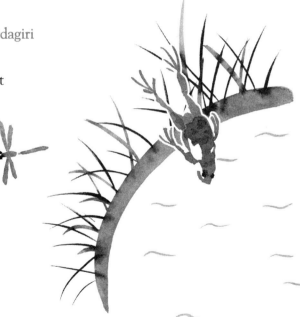

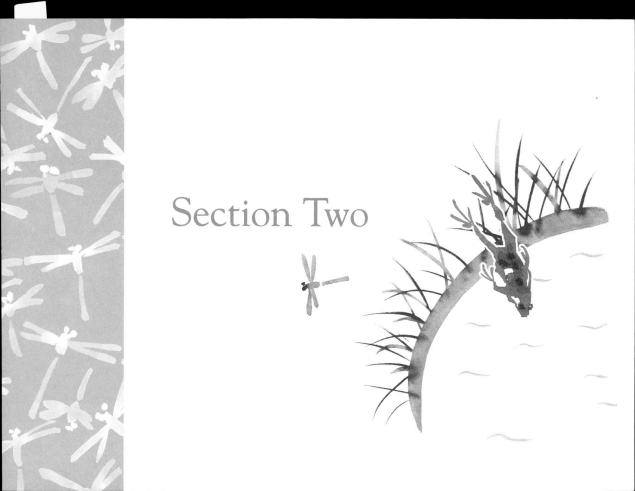

Section Two

Yoko Danno

> Old-pond—a frog
> leaps in
> water sound

Bill Deemer

HIGH KUKU

> I enlightened Bashō,
> recalled the Frog,
> but he scared me!

Bernard Lionel Einbond

Antic pond—
frantic frog jumps in—
gigantic sound.

Into an old pond,
a leaping frog tumbles—
the sound of water.

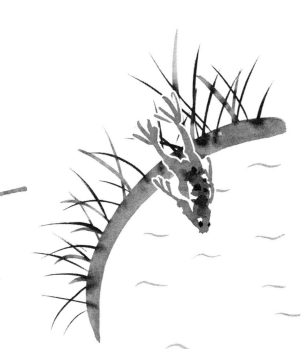

An old pond—
a frog tumbles in—
the water's sound.

from "Insomnia in Haiku Form"
16

Unable to sleep—
I imagine an old pond,
and a frog jumps in.

Robert Anthony Fagan

from "Travels"

> hey
> the frog's fallen
> in the pond
> splash

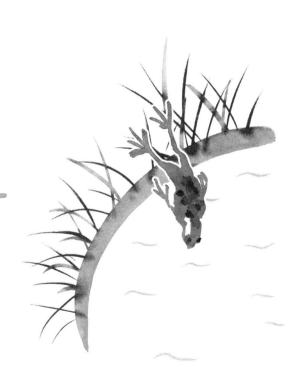

Ross Figgins

Some Notes on the Old Pond

1. After working with this for a while, I can't resist a pun. I don't
    know the legitimacy of word plays in translation, but . . .

    > old pond,
    > frog jumps in—
    >   a sound question

2. The next is an attempt to capture the sound by bracketing it
    between the interrupted moments of silence. The ambiguity is
    intended.

    > old pond,
    > a frog leaps in—
    >   a moment after, silence

3. And finally a more literal interpretation.

> old pond—
> the sound
> of a frog and water

Wm Flygare

transliteration

. . . old . . pond . . .
. . . frog . leap . . .
. . . water sound . . .

transvisions

stillness . . .
a frog-pond ploomp!
makes it breathe.

the universe . . .   ab-sence   (samsara)
a froglet moves it   bare attention   (satipatthana)
listen! . . . . . .   presence   (nirvana)

silent mystery . .   dead pond
a tiny frog   tiny frog
sounds its depths.   live mind

the wordless Word: nay
a frog-pond plop   yea
makes it heard.   aye
                          ?
                          !
                          .

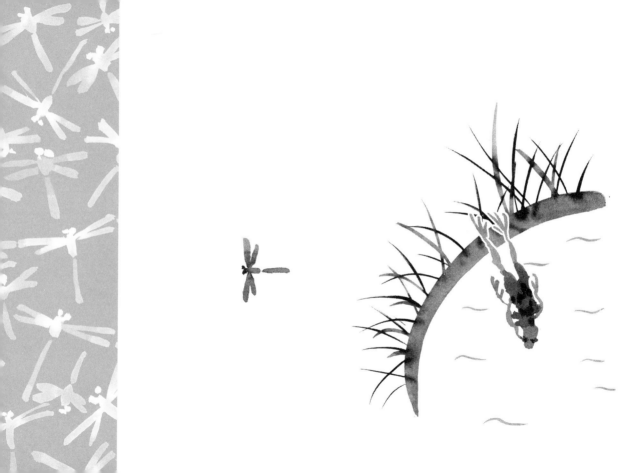

bearded pond,
tickled by frog,
says, "ugh!" . . . & smiles.

my mind was still
till Bashō's frog
made it ripple.

pond plus frog is what?:
splash? plash? or plop?
ploop? ploomp? or flop?

Lorraine Ellis Harr

The quiet pond;
And a frog jumps
Splash!

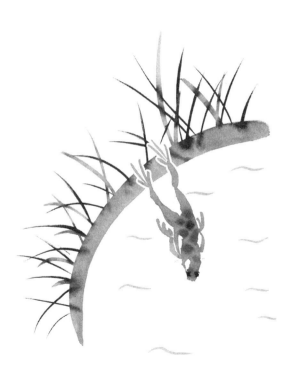

The old pond:
  A frog jumps into it—
        Plip/plop

Quiet pond:
        Frog-jump-in
                Plop-sound.

A quiet pond;
  A frog jumps
          kersplat!

Blip!
    A frog plunges
              into the pond.

Mossy pond:
  Plunging frog's
            water-blip.

Quiet old pool:
            Blip!
a frog jumps-in.

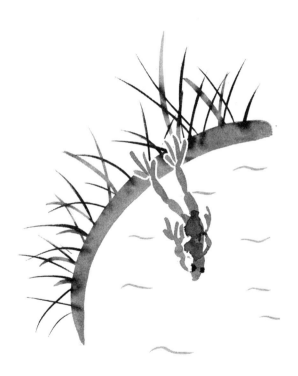

Water-gluck:
Into the old pond
             a frog jumps

Old mossy pond;
a frog jumps
             blip/splat

Blip/splat!
Into the old mossy pond
             a frog jumps—

Lindley Williams Hubbell

I've made two tries:

> An old pond
> A frog jumping
> Sound of water

but after reading Curtis Hidden Page I felt that my version was terribly unpoetical, so I tried again:

> Oh thou unrippled pool of quietness
> Upon whose shimmering surface, like the tears
> Of olden days, a small batrachian leaps,
> The while aquatic sounds assail our ears.

Hisao Kanaseki

an old pond:
noises of frogs
leaping in

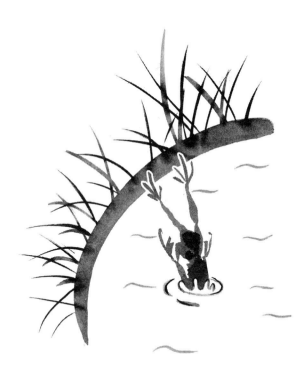

James Kirkup

Age-old pond stillness.
Jump of a frog disturbs it
With a little plop.

pond
    frog
        plop!

Frank Kuenstler

from *EMPIRE*

> Once upon a time there was a frog
> Once upon a time there was a pond
> *Splash.*

William Matheson

from "Ten Variations on Bashō's 'Pond and Frog' *Haiku*"

III

Jumpe, jumpe, lyttle Frogge!
Water soundeth
All aroundeth
In thyss olde Bogge.

VIII

———ah vecchio stagno———
———una rana ha saltato
. . . dell'acqua il suono . . .

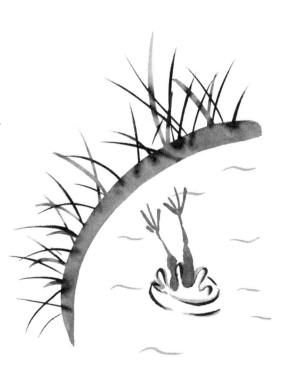

X

"And what, after all," she paused, as if taking advantage—which he knew (oh, yes! he knew) she *was*, by heaven!, doing—of the last of the October light so parsimoniously, and yet with such prodigality, such largesse, being filtered into the room through the window giving on to the Park (but such squalid little panes! he could not help himself—and considering everything, considering particularly *this* thing, why *should* he help himself—from thinking), "did, as you seemingly want to tell me about it, 'happen,'—I believe that was how you expressed it?"

"Well," he began, with every intention of holding it up, confound it!; it was now, or, to coin a phrase, never.

"Well'?" she held fire and there it was, in all its shabby, its commercial, glory, glittering and luminous, between them. "Only 'well'?"

"Well," taking a perverse delight in the slowness of his enunciation, as how often, God only knows, these last months, *she* had and over matters infinitely less, to her but unfortunately not to him, important, "there was a noise, a sound, an echo, one might say."

"One 'might,' but should one, should particularly *you*, say so?"

"Oh, well, I, for all that. . . ." She sailed beyond his modest disclaimer, as she always managed, somehow, and in spite of what were to her, at least, genuine feelings of respect—if that was what he wanted—for him, to do. "And," she continued, she so invincibly continued, contriving in some fashion, out of some font of charity, some well-spring of *tendresse*, to give him, if not breathing-space, at least time to take a turn around the, he thought, wretched little *chambre de bonne* which she had the pretension to call—and the miracle of it was, had had the force, or merely the cleverness, of character to cause others to call—a "salon," "this 'noise,' this 'sound,' what exactly, if you'll allow me the indiscretion, *was* it? What, if I may be so bold to ask, *made* it?"

"Ah, as to the making of it, and I think it charming, *en dernière analyse*, for you to use the word, when all is said and done," knowing, as he full well *did* know, that nothing, indeed, had been said or done, that nearly nothing had even begun being "said" and that, there being worlds still to be said, surely nothing could even be considered as being "done," "that's

"One 'might,' but should one, should particularly *you*, say so?"

"Oh, well, I, for all that. . . ." She sailed beyond his modest disclaimer, as she always managed, somehow, and in spite of what were to her, at least, genuine feelings of respect—if that was what he wanted—for him, to do. "And," she continued, she so invincibly continued, contriving in some fashion, out of some font of charity, some well-spring of *tendresse*, to give him, if not breathing-space, at least time to take a turn around the, he thought, wretched little *chambre de bonne* which she had the pretension to call—and the miracle of it was, had had the force, or merely the cleverness, of character to cause others to call—a "salon," "this 'noise,' this 'sound,' what exactly, if you'll allow me the indiscretion, *was* it? What, if I may be so bold to ask, *made* it?"

"Ah, as to the making of it, and I think it charming, *en dernière analyse*, for you to use the word, when all is said and done," knowing, as he full well *did* know, that nothing, indeed, had been said or done, that nearly nothing had even begun being "said" and that, there being worlds still to be said, surely nothing could even be considered as being "done," "that's

a relatively simple matter: it jumped, or leapt, or threw itself, or was propelled—*le choix est à vous*—into it, and consequently, as such is often the case, it made a noise."

"I hope you don't, after all these years, find me—it would be shocking, my love if you *did*, but these things happen—benighted or unenlightened, or simply deficient, but," her fine (as fine as in Florence) eyes searched vaguely for his, as though this were the last of her beacons, the last of all harbors in which to anchor her craft, "if you'll permit me, what 'jumped' into what and what made what 'noise'?"

"Ah, *there*, my dear, you have it, *all* of it. Or, rather, wouldn't you say?, we *both* have it, all of it, in all its little quivering, tremulous, so preciously ephemeral, being?"

I cannot say, precisely, that *I* have it, but I am comforted, if that is the word, by *your* having it, having it so utterly yours, as you have always had," her face in the nearly posthumous effulgence of twilight turning slowly, and as if for the last, the desperately last, time, from his, "everything."

R. Clarence Matsuo-Allard

ancient pond—
a frog jumping into its splash

Clare Nikt

Hear the lively song
of the frog in
BrrrBrrrBrrptyBrrrBrrrrrrrrrIp.
Plash !

Michael O'Brien

My Noble Lord:
The cat just pissed on the Basho translations.
O ancient lake!

Michael O'Brien

The Origin of Haiku

for Bashō

The little frog   lost his footing

Ron Padgett

"Advertising translation"

old pond
frog jumps in
plop plop fizz fizz

Cyril Patterson

Without pondering its next leap,
   a bullfrog makes its splash!

The spirit
of the old pond is
frog-bound.

A	a
pon	fat
der	old
ous	frog
oc	goes
ca	
sion	plop!

Finality—
a bullfrog croaks beside
the lily pond.

Zen leap—
a bullfrog makes its
splash!

Without pondering
its next leap,
a bullfrog makes its
splash!

One frog flattened
on the road—
another croaks beside
the lily pond.

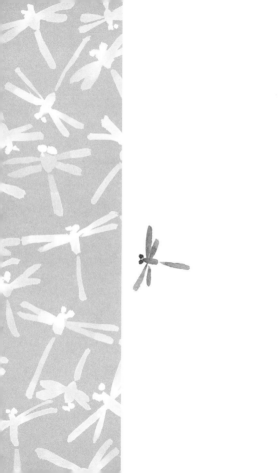

From the pond's edge,
a bullfrog PLOPS into
oblivion.

Barbara Ruch

An old green pond.
A small green frog dives in.
The ping of water.

Eleanor Wolff

Age-old pool ya
A frog jumps into
the water: the sound of it

Old old pond ya
Sound, as a frog jumps in,
of water . . . .

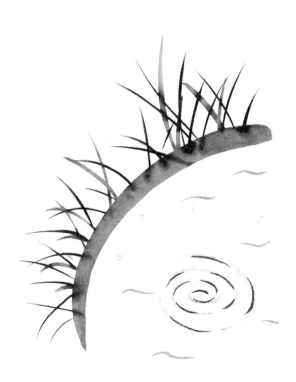

George M. Young, Jr.

After perusing *Basho's Furuike*, I checked, and sure enough found in my file of yellowed newspaper clippings the following notice:

MAFIA HIT MAN POET: NOTE FOUND PINNED TO LAPEL OF DROWNED VICTIM'S DOUBLE-BREASTED SUIT! ! ! ! !

> Dere wasa dis frogg
> Gone jumpa offa da logg
> Now he inna bogg.
>   —Anonymous

According to the newspaper account, neither the author's victim nor the victim's identity has yet been ascertained.

Thought you might be interested in this strange item—another wrinkle to the age-old mystery of the frog and the pond.

Epilogue

Voices of frogs
As if to accompany
All those stars
—Eleanor Wolff

Sources and Credits

Aitken, Robert. *Blind Donkey*, 1 (1975): 1-2. Reprinted with permission.

———. *A Zen Wave: Bashō's Haiku & Zen*. Tokyo: John Weatherhill, 1978. Reprinted with permission.

Akimoto, Shunkichi. *Exploring the Japanese Ways of Life*. Tokyo: Tokyo News Service, 1961. Reprinted with permission.

Alexander, Scott. *Haiku West* 1, no. 1 (June 1967). Attempts to get in touch with the author were futile.

Anonymous. "Haiku and the West . . . ," *The Times Educational Supplement*, March 20, 1959. Reprinted with permission of Times Newspapers.

Anonymous. *Don't Tell the Scarecrow*. New York: Scholastic Book Services, 1969. Attempts to identify the translator were fruitless. Reprinted with permission of the publisher.

Aston, W. G. *A History of Japanese Literature*. New York: D. Appleton Century, 1899.

Behn, Harry. *Cricket Songs: Japanese Haiku*. New York: Harcourt Brace Jovanovich, 1964. Reprinted with permission.

Beilenson, Peter, *Japanese Haiku*. Mount Vernon, New York: Peter Pauper Press, 1956. Reprinted with permission. A version with the same word-ing, but arranged in three lines and aligned at left, appears in his *Lotus Blossoms* (New York: Peter Pauper Press, 1970).

Beilenson, Peter, and Behn, Harry. *Haiku Harvest*. Mount Vernon, New York: Peter Pauper Press, 1962. Reprinted with permission.

Blyth, R. H. *Zen in English Literature and Oriental Classics*. Tokyo: Hokuseido Press, 1942. Reprinted with permission.

———. *Haiku*, vol. 1. Tokyo: Hokuseido Press, 1949. Reprinted with permission.

Bond, Edward. *Narrow Road to the Deep North*. New York: Hill & Wang, 1969. Reprinted with permission of Farrar, Strauss & Giroux.

Bownas, Geoffrey, and Thwaite, Anthony. *The Penguin Book of Japanese Verse*. Harmondsworth, Middlesex: Penguin Books, 1964. © Geoffrey Bownas and Anthony Thwaite. Reprinted with permission.

Britton, Dorothy. *A Haiku Journey: Bashō's "The Narrow Road to the Far North" and Selected Haiku*. Tokyo: Kodansha International, 1974. Reprinted with permission.

Brower, Robert H. "Japanese," *Versification: Major Language Types*. Edited by W. K. Wimsatt. New York: New York University Press, 1972. Reprinted with permission.

Bryan, John Thomas. *The Literature of Japan*. New York: Kennikat Press, 1929. Attempts to get permission were fruitless.

Buchanan, Daniel C. *One Hundred Famous Haiku*. San Francisco: Japan Publications, 1973. Attempts to get permission were fruitless.

Cassedy, Sylvia, and Kunihiro, Suetake. *Birds, Frogs, and Moonlight*. New York: Doubleday & Co., 1967. Reprinted with permission.

Chamberlain, Basil Hall. "Bashō and the Japanese Poetical Epigram," *Transactions of the Asiatic Society of Japan* 30, no. 2 (1902). From the typographical arrangement, Chamberlain seems to have intended this as a "literal" translation, rather than a "poetic" one.'

Cohen, William Howard. *To Walk in Seasons*. Tokyo: Charles E. Tuttle Co., 1972. Reprinted with permission.

Corman, Cid. *Cool Gang*. Ashland, Massachusetts: Origin Press, 1959. Reprinted with permission.

Emerson, Gertrude. "Haikai Poetry," *The Forum* 51 (March 1914).

Fraser, G. S. "The Frog and the Pond: First Steps in Japanese Poetics," *Nine* 3, no. 4, whole no. 9 (Summer–Autumn 1952). Attempts to get permission were futile.

———. *Metre, Rhyme and Free Verse*. London: Methuen, 1970. Attempts to get permission led nowhere.

Ginsberg, Allen. *The New York Times*, February 16, 1979. Ginsberg has a poem of fourteen quatrains, *Old Pond*, beginning with the line, "The old pond—a frog jumps in, kerplunk!" in *Zero* 2 (1979).

Giroux, Joan. *The Haiku Form*. Tokyo: Charles E. Tuttle Co., 1974. Reprinted with permission.

Hearn, Lafcadio. *Exotics and Retrospectives in Ghostly Japan*. Boston: Little, Brown & Co. 1898. In the Charles E. Tuttle Co. reprint of the book, the translation appears as "Old pond—frogs jumping in—sound of water."

Henderson, Harold G. "Haiku—Ancient and Modern," *Asia* 24 (February 1934).

———. *An Introduction to Haiku*. New York: Doubleday & Co., 1958. Reprinted with permission.

Higginson, William J. *Itadakimasu*. Kanona, New York: J & C Transcripts, 1971. Reprinted with permission.

Ibanez, Felix-Marti. "The Time Talisman," Chanoyu Quarterly, no. 13 (1976). Reprinted with permission of the Uransenke Foundation.

Ikeda, Kenjun. "English haiku no mondai-ten," *Minerva*, no. 2 (1972). Attempts to get permission were futile.

Janeira, Armando Martins. *Japanese and Western Literature*. Tokyo: Charles E. Tuttle Co., 1970. Reprinted with permission.

Keene, Donald. *Japanese Literature: An Introduction for Western Readers*. New York: Grove Press, 1955. Reprinted with permission. The second version appears in three lines, aligned at left and with a slight typo-graphical variation, in his *World Within Walls* (New York: Holt, Rinehart & Winston, 1976).

Maeda, Cana. "On Translating the *Haiku* Form," *Harvard Journal of Asiatic Studies* 29 (1969). Reprinted with permission of the editors of the *Journal*.

Marks, Alfred H. "Haiku in Japanese and English," *Chanoyu Quarterly*, no. 9 (1974). Reprinted with permission of the Uransenke Foundation.

Masaoka, Shiki. *Shiki Zenshū*, vol. 4. Tokyo: Kodansha, 1978. This translation appears in Shiki's college paper in English, "Baseo as a Poet," which is thought to have been written in 1892.

Miner, Earl. *Japanese Linked Poetry*. Princeton: Princeton University Press, 1979. Reprinted with permission.

Miner, Earl, and Odagiri, Hiroko. *The Monkey's Straw Raincoat*. Princeton: Princeton University Press, 1981. Reprinted with permission.

Miyamori, Asataro. *One Thousand Haiku Ancient and Modern*. Tokyo: Dobunsha, 1930.

———. *An Anthology of Haiku Ancient and Modern*. Tokyo: Maruzen, 1932.

Nippon Gakujutsu Shinkōkai. *Haikai and Haiku*. Tokyo: Nippon Gakujutsu Shinkōkai, 1958. Reprinted with permission.

Nitobe, Inazo. *Japanese Traits and Foreign Influences*. London: Trubner, 1927.

———. *Lectures on Japan*. Tokyo: Kenkyusha,1936.

Noguchi, Yone. *The Spirit of Japanese Poetry*. London: John Murray, 1914.

O'Donnol, Dion. "One sheet (green) printing of 'the frog poem' as used in my poetry classes in the 1963–1969 period" (as described by the author). Reprinted with author's permission.

———. "Splash, Classical Japanese Haiku, Englished by Dion O'Donnol" (1968). Reprinted with author's permission.

Otake, Masaru V. "The Haiku Touch in Wallace Stevens and Some Imagists," *East–West Review* 2, no. 2 (Winter 1965–66). Reprinted with permission.

Page, Curtis Hidden. *Japanese Poetry, an historical essay*. Boston: Houghton Mifflin, 1923. Reprinted with permission of the Estate of Curtis Hidden Page.

Porter, William J. *A Year of Japanese Epigrams*. London: Oxford University Press, 1911. Reprinted with permission.

Saisho, Fumiko. "A Few Notes on 'Haikai' and the Japanese Mind," *Cultural Nippon* 3, no. 2 (June 1935). Attempts to get permission led nowhere.

Saito, Hidesaburo. As cited in Miyamori's *Anthology* (which see).Seidensticker, Edward G., and Nasu, Kiyoshi. *Nihongo-rashii Hyōgen kara Eigo-rashii Hyōgen e*. Tokyo: Baifūkan, 1962. Reprinted with permission.

Stewart, Harold. *A Net of Fireflies*. Tokyo: Charles E. Tuttle Co., 1960. Reprinted with permission.

Stryk, Lucien, and Ikemoto, Takashi. *Haiku of the Japanese Masters*. Derry, Pennsylvania: The Rook Press, 1977. The translation also appears in *The Penguin Book of Zen Poetry* (New York: Viking/Penguin, 1981). Reprinted with permission.

Suzuki, Daisetz T. "Zen and Japanese Poetry," *Contemporary Japan* 10, no. 4 (April 1941).
———. *Zen and Japanese Culture*. Princeton: Princeton University Press, 1959. Reprinted with permission.

Takamine, Hiroshi. "Love and Haiku," *Today's Japan* 13, no. 9 (September 1958). Attempts to get permission led nowhere.

Toyoda, Minoru. As cited in Miyamori's Anthology (which see). Ueda, Makoto. *Matsuo Bashō*. New York: Twayne Publishers, 1970. Reprinted with permission of G. K. Hall.

Walsh, Clara A. *The Master-Singers of Japan*. London: John Murray, 1910.

Yasuda, Kenneth. *A Pepper Pod*. New York: Alfred A. Knopf, 1947. Reprinted with permission of Charles E. Tuttle Co.

Yuasa, Nobuyuki. *Basho: The Narrow Road to the Deep North and Other Travel Sketches*. Harmondsworth, Middlesex: Penguin Books, 1966. © Nobuyuki Yuasa. Reprinted with permission.

Inklings Editions are a production of Weatherhill, Inc., publishers of fine books on Asia and the Pacific. Editorial supervision: Jeffrey Hunter. Book and cover design: Mariana Canelo Francis. Production supervision: Bill Rose. Printing and binding: Daamen Printing, West Rutland, Vermont.